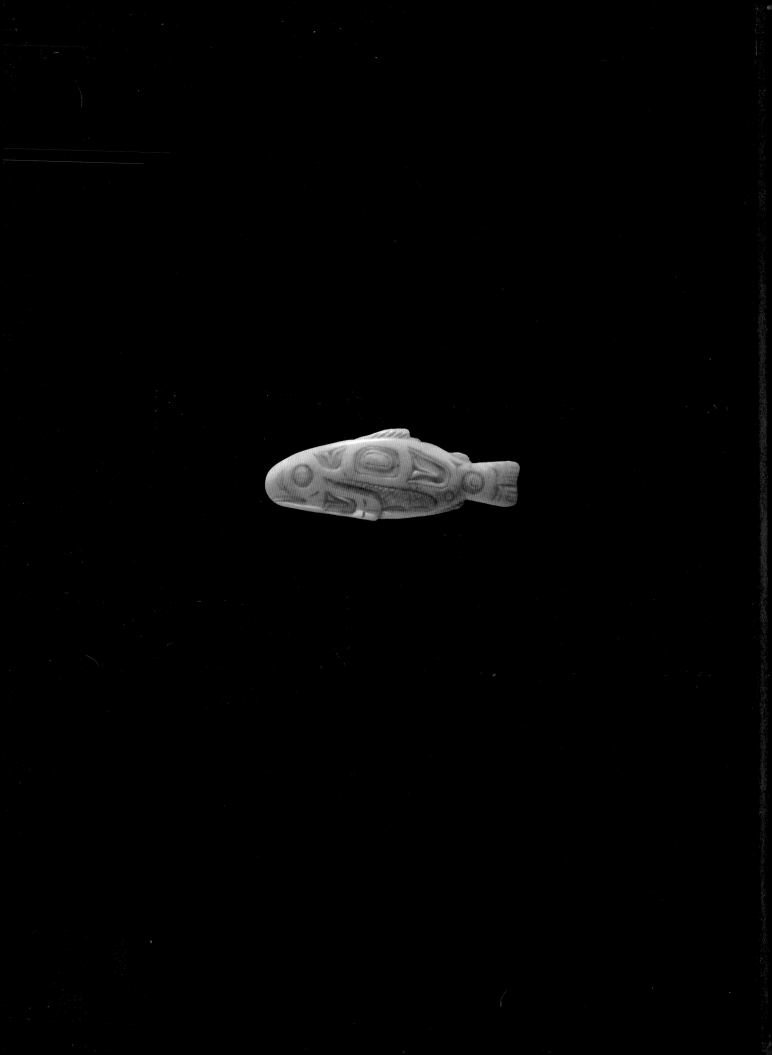

The Prince *and the* Salmon People

RIZZOLI
NEW YORK

retold by Claire Rudolf Murphy   *illustrated by* Duane Pasco

LONG ago, in a village surrounded by snow capped mountains and lush green forests, there lived a Tsimshian Indian chief and his wife, who was nearing her time to deliver their first child.

The day she bore the prince, shouts of joy were heard throughout the village—and by the river, too, for at the very moment of the boy's birth, the first spring salmon of the season swam up the river and into the fishermen's nets.

Niawas-ye, the greatest of all shamans, performed the First Salmon Ritual by the river. He prepared the fish, laying it out on a cedar mat. Then four old shamans carried the salmon on the mat, following Niawas-ye up to the village. When the procession stopped in front of the village chief's house, the chief held up his new baby for all to see. The villagers cheered and clapped for their new prince.

Niawas-ye shook his rattle, blessing the child: "This boy is special. He enters our world just as the first spring salmon comes to us. He will bring a great gift to our people; he will remind us how important it is to respect and honor the salmon."

Later, the shaman placed a necklace with a salmon charm around the baby's neck.

A village chief's job was to monitor the effects of nature and weather on his people, mediate at council with local house chiefs, and preside over winter ceremonies. Above, Chief Stiaowax of the Nishga (Tsimshian) appears in full chief's regalia, c. 1900. He wears a Chilkat robe, a woven wool garment that possibly originated among the Tsimshian, and was later perfected by another tribe, the Tlingit. Right, this Tlingit Chilkat robe, c. 1850, is made of mountain-goat wool, yellow cedar bark, commercial yarn, dye pigments.

Northwest Coast tribes had distinct classes of people. For example, children of nobility inherited special privileges and grew up to be village leaders. They also learned lore and behavior concerning ceremonial activities. The commoners were like the middle class of today. Slaves, about a third of the population, were usually captured from other tribes or were children of slaves. Above: photo by Benjamin Haldane, Royal British Columbia Museum, #PN4329; right: Chilkat robe, Seattle Art Museum, photo by Paul Macapia.

When the prince grew older he wore his necklace every year during the season of the First Salmon, and the runs were plentiful. He and his companion, a slave boy whom the chief appointed to stay with him, watched the men fishing and longed to join them.

Years went by and life in the village became busier. Some rituals were performed less often or not at all. Gradually the prince forgot to wear his necklace, until one day he couldn't even remember where he had put it. That year he and his companion were finally old enough to catch spring salmon with the men, but almost no fish swam by the village.

In the winter the villagers starved. Every day the chief and his wife went into the woods with their people to scrape the tree sap underneath the bark for nourishment.

One day the prince and his companion stayed at home and made arrows. After a while the slave boy started crying because he was hungry. So the prince looked around the house for something his friend could eat. He found many of his mother's food boxes, but they were all empty. Finally, he untied and opened a large painted box with a small box inside. The smaller box contained a large dried spring salmon, all folded up. The prince cut a small piece off the huge fish, fed it to his friend, and then put the rest away.

Clockwise from left: This large, lidded Bentwood box is a masterpiece in wood technology. Its sides were formed of a single plank of cedar, which was bent to form three of its corners. The fourth corner was made by joining the plank's ends. Bentwood objects can be as large as storage chests, or small enough to hold in the palm of your hand. This medium-sized Bentwood bowl, below, could be held in your arms. Lower left, this is a graceful twined basket woven of cedar bark and decorated with dyed bear grass. All of these household objects are Tsimshian, Thomas Burke Memorial Washington State Museum.

His parents returned late that evening with the fresh sap they had gathered. Immediately his mother went to the large box, untied it, and opened the small box.

"Who has stolen my salmon?" she shouted when she discovered the missing piece. "This is all the dried salmon I have. I've been saving it for two years."

Finally the prince answered, "I did, Mother."

"Oh. . . !" said his mother, shaking him, for she was as angry as fire. "You did not care about helping us gather food today. Yet now you are hungry and begin to steal!"

"I did not eat any of it myself," said the prince, starting to cry. "I felt sorry for my companion, who was so hungry he cried all day after you left. So I went looking for food and when I found your salmon, I fed him a small portion."

But the mother would not listen and continued to scold her son. When the prince could take it no longer, he left the house.

He spoke to his friend, who waited outside. "Get my marten cloak for me, for I am going to leave my mother's house. You stay behind and look after my parents."

The prince put on his marten garment and began to walk a long ways in the woods along the river bank. After many miles, he stopped and felt the pockets of his cloak. They were filled with mountain-goat fat. He smiled, knowing he would not go hungry, thanks to his friend. Reaching into another pocket he discovered his lost salmon necklace. He put it around his neck and continued to walk.

After a while, the slave boy became so sad that he started crying loudly. The chief came out and asked, "Why do you cry so?"

"My young master went away from home."

"Quick—tell the rest of the village."

So the prince's companion walked around, shouting, "My master has gone away from home tonight, great village!" And soon all the villagers came out carrying bark torches. They searched all night for the prince but could not find him.

These Tenaktak (Kwakiutl) canoes are similar in style to the Tsimshian's ocean-going canoes. Photo by Edward Curtis, (#74718) British Columbia Archives and Records Service.

From a distance the prince saw lights and heard voices, but he ignored them and continued walking. Finally, when he was very tired, he sat down and rested against a tree.

After a long while he heard the sound of distant paddling on the water. Moments later a canoe landed below him and a voice said, "It is here that we will find him, at the foot of the big tree."

Four men walked up the bank to where the prince sat. Then one of them said, "Well, dear little man, one of your uncles has been ill for two years, but today you gave him relief. Because of this he wants you to visit him."

Since he always did what his uncles told him, the prince climbed into the beautiful canoe, adorned with carved and painted salmon at its bow and stern.

The steersman said, "Now lie down and rest." And as the men began paddling, the boy fell fast asleep.

The young prince awoke when the canoe landed on a sandy beach in front of a large village where children were playing. The cedar houses were decorated with carved figures of spring salmon. In the middle of the village stood a very large house adorned with a huge carved spring salmon. The fish was painted so brightly that the prince thought it was real.

Meanwhile, several men ran to meet the boat. They were tall and strong, dressed in colorful robes with red linings. They called to him, "Here, Prince. Here, master. Your uncle, the chief, has long expected you."

They accompanied the prince from the beach to the big cedar-plank house. Inside, at the back of the house, the great chief lay stretched out on a mat before a fire, not moving because he was paralyzed.

His uncle spoke to his attendants in a great voice. "Spread out a mat on which my nephew may sit."

As soon as the prince did so, a little old woman appeared at his side and spoke to him. "Do you know who I am?" The prince shook his head. "Ah, that's right. Your elders have forgotten to pass on the stories and honor the rituals." The little old woman stared at the prince. "You should know that I am Mouse Woman."

The prince nodded. He remembered that once when he was little his grandfather, the chief, told a story about how Mouse Woman helped a woman who had turned into a bear.

"I am a spirit who can appear as a mouse or as the tiniest of grandmothers. And for a payment I will help humans who find themselves in the animal world—as you have."

"But what will I give you?" the prince asked, confused.

"Isn't that mountain-goat fat in your garment there?" The boy nodded.

"That will do just fine." Mouse Woman took the fat and began chewing it. She chose her next words with care.

"Your people believe that animals have bodies and spirits just like humans, and can go back and forth between the human and animal worlds. They know that animals such as the Salmon People live under the ocean in their own houses."

Cedar-plank houses were impressive structures. The chief's house could be as large as forty by sixty feet, but could be much larger. A typical house had four interior posts (often carved with decorations). Overlapping planks were placed on top of the rafters to make the roof, leaving a smoke hole in the middle. The interior included a large excavated area in the middle for the hearth with platforms around its perimeter to serve as living quarters. The head of the family or the chief occupied the quarters along the back wall opposite the entrance. The housefront was often painted with the crest of the house chief who lived there, usually with a character from the origin myth of the chief's lineage. Above, a Tsimshian killer whale housefront, c. 1875, Port Simpson, British Columbia, Smithsonian Institution. Left, a model of a cedar-plank house depicts a grizzly bear on its housefront, Thomas Burke Memorial Washington State Museum.

The prince opened his eyes wide, remembering the carvings on the houses. "I have been brought to the Spring Salmon People's world?"

Mouse Woman nodded. "I must tell you, the Salmon People will visit your village only if they are treated well. In the past, your people have honored them in rituals. But these are now forgotten, just as I am forgotten. Your people go hungry because they no longer respect that there are spirits in all things. Because of this, the Salmon People feel no obligation to feed the human world."

Just then the Chief of the Spring Salmon People called out, "It is good that you are here, Prince, so we can teach you our ways and you can take them back to your people. I have suffered a long time because your mother hoarded me in her food box. The other day I felt so relieved when you spread me out. Thank you."

The boy moved closer when his uncle's voice faded to a whisper. "Your mother should not have kept me folded up for two years. All dried salmon must be eaten within one year." The chief tried to reach out and touch his nephew, but he could not move.

"You shall live with me in my own house while you learn our ways. Then, when it is time, we will return with you to your home."

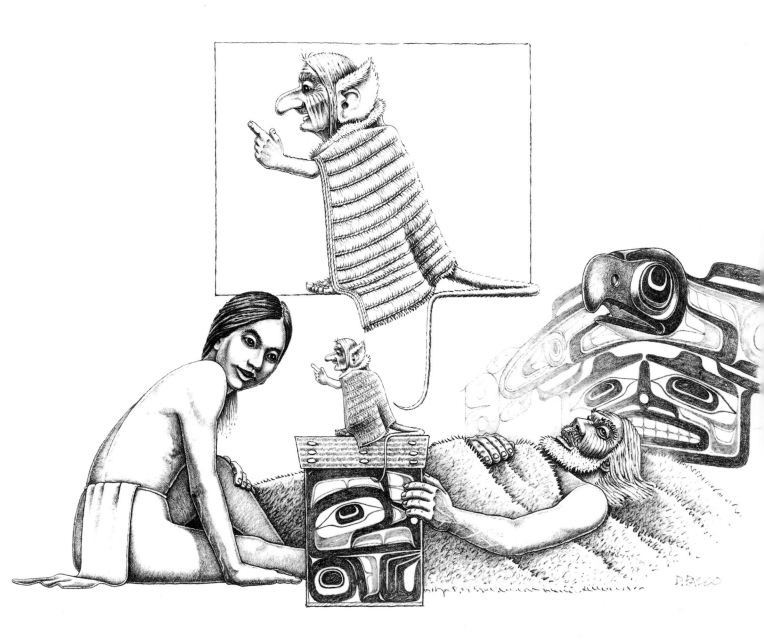

Northwest Coast Indians believed that salmon were people in another form who lived in villages beneath the sea. Every year the Salmon People exchanged their outer human garments for those of fish and migrated upstream to offer themselves as food to the humans or die after spawning. In either event the salmon's bones were returned to the water and floated back to sea, where they were transformed into living Salmon People.

Salmon was the mainstay for tribes like the Tsimshian. The Salmon People legend interprets the cyclical flow of life and death that the Indians witnessed each year with the salmon migrations. Left, Tlingit Salmon People sculptures, approximately seventeen inches tall, Lowie Museum of Anthropology, University of California at Berkeley, photo by Peter T. Furst.

The next day the prince walked around the village. Mouse Woman again appeared by his side and whispered in his ear. "See these children playing? They look human, but they are really little salmon. If you are hungry, touch one of them on the head and the child will turn into a fish, ready to feed you."

The prince was startled and shook his head. But Mouse Woman reassured him, explaining, "You are in the world of the Salmon People. All of the villagers here are really fish. They know that if you honor them with the rituals and take care of their remains after you eat them, they will come back to life and swim back to their home."

The prince walked a while longer, but soon his stomach began to growl. Just then a little boy came up to him, saying, "You are hungry. Let me feed you. Then you will help me swim in the river again."

Remembering all that Mouse Woman had told him, the prince touched the boy on the head and the child turned into a large spring salmon.

Suddenly Mouse Woman was at the prince's side.
"Now I will instruct you in the proper care of the salmon.
First, clean out its insides and then toast the flesh over
the fire. When you are finished eating, gather all the
bones and remnants, throw them in the river, and then
drink your fill of water. If you do this correctly, the salmon
will be able to swim back to its home."

The prince did as Mouse Woman told him. He ate the
salmon, returned its bones to the river, and drank his fill
of water. Satisfied, he went back to his uncle's house. As

he approached the house he heard a child's painful cries. "Oh, my eye is sore! My eye is sore!"

"You are the cause of his suffering," Mouse Woman told the prince when he entered. "Go and search in the hole at the foot of your roasting spit!"

The prince quickly ran out to the fire and found the eye of the little spring salmon and threw it into the river. Just as he did so, the crying stopped.

After that the prince continued to live with the Salmon People, learning their ways and practicing their rituals.

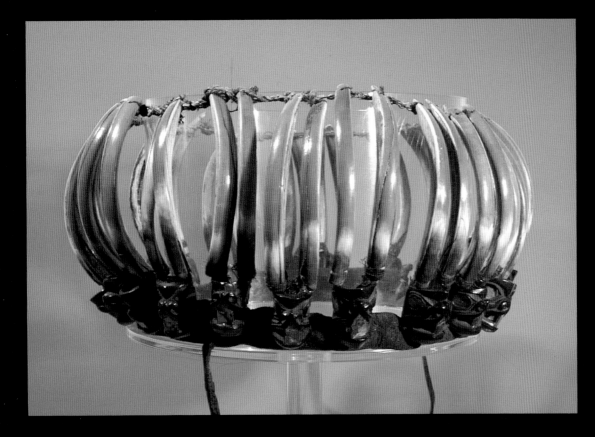

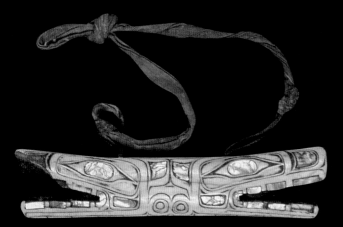

Shamans were holy people or scientists with special knowledge of the physical and spiritual worlds. They communicated with powerful spirits, healed the body, and foretold future events. They were well-paid men and women who had assistants.

In the Tsimshian language, *"Halait"* is the term for shaman. A healing shaman is *"Swansk Halait;" "Swansk"* means healer. This Tsimshian shaman, far left, wears a crown of 22 grizzly bear claws, like the one pictured above. A soul-catcher, like this one, left, is attached to his beaded necklace. Soul catchers were a shaman's most important charm. If a person's sickness was believed to be caused by the soul leaving the body, the shaman would search for the lost soul, enticing it to enter the soul catcher and then returning it to the patient. Or he could use a soul catcher to suck a bad spirit out of a patient. Far left, Tsimshian shaman (#882-25) and soul catcher (#877-254), Canadian Museum of Civilization; Tsimshian shaman crown, private collection, photo by Peter T. Furst.

Back in the Tsimshian village, the chief went up into the hills every day to mourn for his son. He fasted and bathed to purify himself so that the Great Spirit might favor him with the prince's safe return. Finally, in desperation, the chief gathered all the village shamans together, saying, "Tell me whether my son is dead or alive."

The holy men worked their spells, but none learned what happened to the prince. So the chief told his attendants to find Niawas-ye, sending them forth with many gifts of tribute.

Niawas-ye came to the home of the chief. When he entered he put on his painted dancing apron, deerskin leggings, and a bearskin robe. He placed an amulet around his neck and painted red marks on his face. Then he took his rattle in his right hand and held the white tail of an eagle in his left. Niawas-ye started to sing. His companions joined in, beating the skin drums that they held. Finally the great shaman began dancing around the fire.

After Niawas-ye repeated his song four times, he stopped in front of the prince's parents. "Your son is not dead. He is alive and lives in the village of the Spring Salmon People." The parents took comfort in hearing this, while the shaman began to sing and dance around the fire once more.

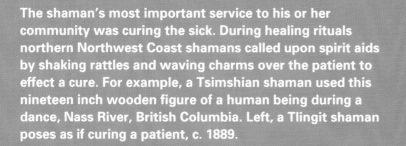

The shaman's most important service to his or her community was curing the sick. During healing rituals northern Northwest Coast shamans called upon spirit aids by shaking rattles and waving charms over the patient to effect a cure. For example, a Tsimshian shaman used this nineteen inch wooden figure of a human being during a dance, Nass River, British Columbia. Left, a Tlingit shaman poses as if curing a patient, c. 1889.

Above, wooden Tsimshian masks like this covered a person's entire face and were worn during ceremonies. Even though the mask looks human it could represent an ancestor or a supernatural spirit in human form. A mask often represented a spirit helper of the person wearing it. Right, Tlingit shaman: #335775, American Museum of Natural History; Tsimshian mask (#3544) and dance figure (#29979), National Museum of the American Indian.

Niawas-ye sang another song four times, then stood still again. "The Spring Salmon People took away your son because your people have not properly cared for them. It is the Spring Salmon Chief that you"—he pointed to the mother—"have kept dried in your food box for two years.

"You must honor the salmon rituals and not keep dried salmon for more than one year. Go now. Eat the entire fish, throw its remnants into the river, and drink your fill of water. Then the Chief of the Spring Salmon will be cured and will return your son to you."

The prince's father and mother did exactly as Niawas-ye said. And as they did so, the Spring Salmon Chief got up off his mat and walked out of his house for the first time in two years. The Salmon People rejoiced.

In the midst of their singing and dancing, scouts returned to the Salmon People's village with news. "Chief, many fresh green cottonwood leaves now grow along the Skeena and Nass rivers. And ice is floating in their currents."

"This is the sign we have been waiting for. It is spring, time for us to move," the great chief told his tribesmen. Then, turning to those who still suffered, he added, "Unfortunately, those of you who are injured will not swim with us this year. If humans do not care for us, we cannot return to them."

Carved conical clan hats like this Tsimshian one, below, featured the clan's crest animal and were passed from generation to generation as supernatural treasures. This one depicts a killer whale. On the preceding page, in Duane Pasco's illustration, the Chief of the Salmon People wears a salmon clan hat. He also wears leggings, similar to the ones pictured below. These leggings, c. 1900, have appliques of fish made of wool trade cloth, fringe of moose skin leather, and decorated with puffin bills. Photo by Eduardo Calderon, Thomas Burke Memorial Washington State Museum; killer whale hat (#3366), National Museum of the American Indian.

Those able to go gathered their cloaks of fish scales, wrapping them around their bodies. Then they climbed into their canoes. When they were ready to set out, the Spring Salmon Chief took a small round pebble from his own mouth and handed it to the prince. "Here—put this in your mouth. It will keep you from growing hungry on our journey."

In the Tsimshian village, Niawas-ye returned to the chief's house and announced, "I have seen in a vision the Chief of the Spring Salmon and his people leaving their village today. The prince is with them. Let all your people fast. Have all the old women work on the salmon nets and the old men make new poles. We must also ready our fishing platforms on the steep rocks along the canyon's walls."

The chief instructed his people to follow the shaman's instructions.

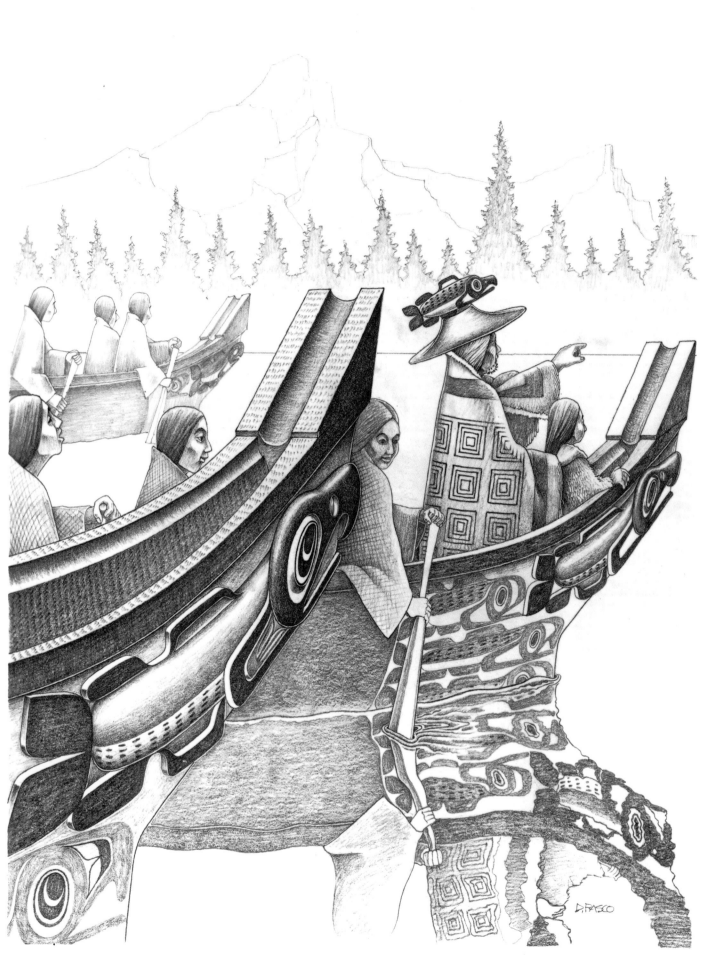

Meanwhile, the Spring Salmon People paddled slowly until they came to an island. This was the village of the Sockeye Salmon, where the people were smaller with bright-red skins. The Spring Salmon Chief stopped and told their chief, "There are now many cottonwood leaves along the Skeena and Nass rivers."

"Then we will follow you," said the Sockeye Salmon Chief.

The canoes of the Spring Salmon People traveled under the sea until they came upon another village. Here the people were humpbacked and very small. Their flesh was pink. The Chief of the Spring Salmon told the Humpback Chief about the cottonwood leaves.

"That is good. We will move after the Sockeye Salmon People move. We will follow them."

The Spring Salmon canoes traveled on. After a very long time they reached an island in the middle of the ocean. Here the prince saw beautiful housefronts, painted and carved with the forms and colors of rainbows.

"Where are we?" he asked.

Most salmon in the world today come from five species that live in the coastal waters of the North Pacific Ocean. During the late spring, summer, or autumn, they spawn (lay their eggs) in fresh water after swimming upstream as far as 2,000 miles (3,200 kilometers) from the ocean. Though scientists don't know for sure, some believe that salmon remember the odor of their home river or stream, and follow the scent.

Salmon migrations vary from region to region depending on climate and how far the salmon have to swim to their home rivers. In southeastern Alaska and northern British Columbia, where this legend takes place, the spring salmon (or king salmon) generally migrate in early May. The sockeye come in the beginning of June, the humpback and dog salmon around July 1, and the coho in mid-July. (In northern Alaska and the Pacific Northwest migration times are different.)

Not every species of salmon comes to every river. Some may never have been present or have recently become extinct in a particular river. Top, the Nass River; bottom, photo showing a salmon migration with fish so dense that one could practically cross the river on their backs. Photos by Maximilien Bruggmann.

Mouse Woman appeared and answered, "This is the village of the Dog Salmon. See those garments in front of the houses? The people here all wear beautiful clothes with purple stripes and have big teeth, too."

The Spring Salmon Chief told the Dog Salmon Chief about the good tidings from the Skeena and Nass rivers.

"That is good what you say," said the other chief. "We will follow after the Humpback Salmon have gone a little distance."

After paddling further, the Spring Salmon People came upon the village of the Coho Salmon, where all the people had long noses and silvery skins. They stopped here, too.

"What you say is good," said the Chief of the Coho Salmon. "But we will wait until late in the fall, just before there is ice on the rivers."

The Spring Salmon People moved along slowly, and after two days reached the place where the rivers flowed into the bay. After resting here, the chief stood up in his canoe and said to all his tribe, "This is where we must separate. You know your rivers. Go your way."

And this they did.

The group with the chief and the young prince traveled up the Skeena River. They went up farther and farther until they reached the mouth of the Kitselas Canyon. Here they rested once more.

Niawas-ye saw this in another vision. So he ordered the villagers to make haste, go down to their platforms, and have their nets and poles ready. Meanwhile, the great shaman also stood ready to dip his net in the river.

As the Salmon People began to swim through the canyon, their chief said to his nephew, "We are approaching your village now, so I will take care of you." As his uncle said this, the prince grew very small and suddenly found himself inside the salmon's chest.

The Spring Salmon Chief slowly made his way up through the swift waters that flowed through the narrow canyon cliffs. Then he saw the huge net of the great shaman almost filling the canyon, and he knew his journey was over. He said to the prince, "Don't let your father dry my flesh! Let him invite the people of all ages to eat my flesh at once. Then you must show them how to do the ritual, so I may live again."

Soon, as Niawas-ye felt his net grow so heavy he could not lift it himself, he called his attendants to help him pull it onto the platform. Knowing this was the Chief of the Spring Salmon, Niawas-ye carefully took the fish out of the net and carried it to shore. Then he turned to one of his attendants and said, "Go tell the villagers that I have caught the Chief of the Spring Salmon, who has our prince. Call four old shamans to be my helpers. Also, bring my robes and a new cedar mat."

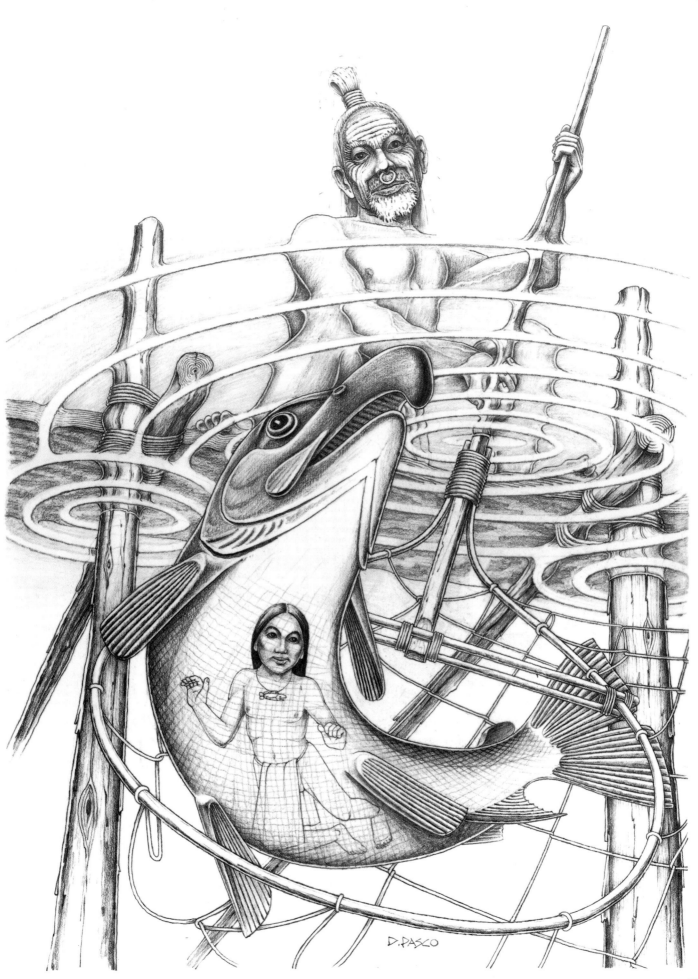

Tsimshian shaman John Lakneets plays a skin drum, c. 1900, like the ones in Duane Pasco's illustrations. His leather apron and the one once worn by a Niska Tsimshian shaman, below, are similar to Niawas-ye's apron in the story. This apron features thirteen ivory halibut charms. Its leather fringe is decorated with dog's teeth and deer hoofs. Left, shaman in dance costume, National Museum of the American Indian; below, apron, Canadian Museum of Civilization, photo by Maximilien Bruggmann.

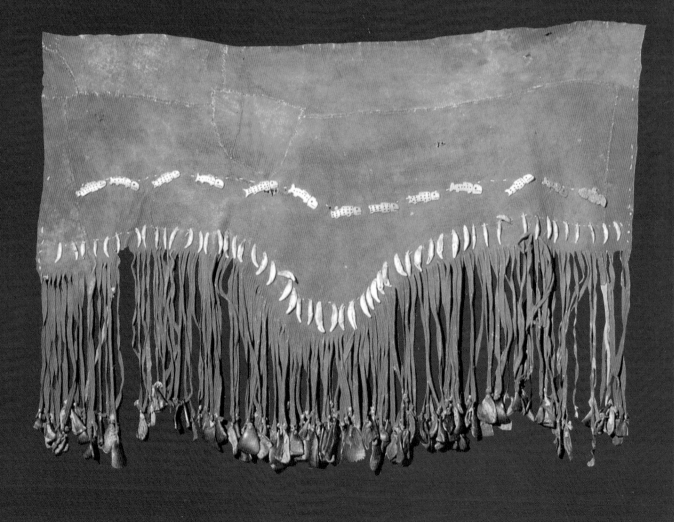

When the four shamans arrived, dressed in their ceremonial clothes, they spread out the mat and placed the salmon on it. Niawas-ye put on his apron, leggings, and his crown of bear claws. The shamans picked up the four corners of the mat and slowly walked up to the village chief's house. The great shaman led the way, shaking his rattle and swinging his eagle tail.

When they reached the house, the shamans went inside and moved the salmon onto a cedar board. Niawas-ye called upon two female shamans to split open the belly of the big spring salmon with their mussel-shell knives. As they cut, they called the salmon by its many names: "My dear Chief of the Spring Salmon, named King Salmon, named Chinook, named Two Gills on Back, named Lightning Following One Another, named Blackmouth, named Three Jumps!"

Then they spread open the fish. Behold! Inside was a child the size of the span from the middle finger to the thumb. And he wore a copper necklace with a carved salmon charm! All the shamans, male and female, pounded their drums and sang as loudly as they could. Niawas-ye danced around the child, shaking his rattle.

The boy began to grow. The shaman kept dancing and dancing, and the child kept growing and growing until he became his normal size. The people saw that it was indeed the prince who had disappeared.

The prince's parents were very happy that their son had returned. They listened as he told stories of how the Spring Salmon People took him to their village and all he learned in their care. He talked about Mouse Woman and told them that the Chief of the Salmon People was also his uncle, who loved him. Finally, he described his journey home and all the Salmon People villages he visited.

"Mother, don't keep dried salmon over a year in your box. Father, whenever we cook fresh salmon, we must throw the bones into the river and drink plenty of water so the salmon can go home. Then they can return to us every spring."

After the chief heard his son's story, he spoke. "We will not forget again, dear Prince. You were born during the First Salmon; now you return to us with the spring salmon. Niawas-ye said at your birth that you were special. You are indeed. I realize now we must always honor the Salmon People."

And as long as the villagers heeded the prince's words, the salmon returned to them every spring and they did not go hungry for many, many years.

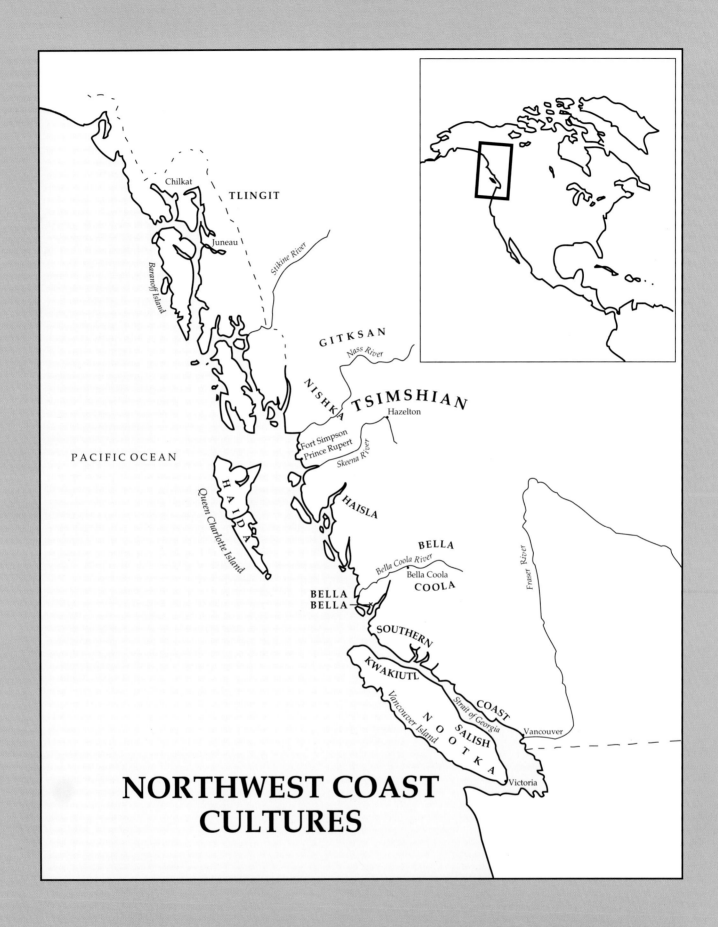

Chilkat

TLINGIT

Juneau

Baranoff Island

Stikine River

GITKSAN

Nass River

NISHKA

TSIMSHIAN

Hazelton

PACIFIC OCEAN

Fort Simpson
Prince Rupert

Skeena River

HAISLA

HAIDA

Queen Charlotte Island

BELLA

Bella Coola River

Bella Coola

COOLA

Fraser River

BELLA
BELLA

SOUTHERN

KWAKIUTL

Vancouver Island

N O O T K A

Strait of Georgia

COAST

SALISH

Vancouver

Victoria

NORTHWEST COAST
CULTURES

DIFFERENT versions of the Salmon People legend have been told for centuries by the many tribes of Northwest Coast Indians, who are interrelated because they travel, trade goods, and share the same climate, wildlife, and vegetation. Though the legend may differ in detail from tribe to tribe, all versions express the Indian belief that animals have spirits, just like people, and can move freely between the animal and human worlds, choosing to feed humans when we respectfully take care of them.

The Tsimshian (Tsim-shan or TSIM-shee-an) are known for their graceful canoes and objects made out of wood, such as totem poles, masks, and carved wooden boxes. In their traditional way of life, the Tsimshian fished, hunted, and lived in groups of families related through the women in large cedar-plank houses built in northwest British Columbia along the Skeena and Nass rivers and, later, in the southeastern Alaska community of Metlakatla.

About 12,000 Tsimshian Indians live in these areas today. They are involved in commercial fishing, logging, commerce, and rekindling their culture by passing on their traditional art forms. Above, a young member of the Tsimshian Eagle Clan performs the Salmon Dance.

Claire Rudolf Murphy spent several years researching this legend because of its powerful, timely message. "Today, salmon face new dangers as they return to their home rivers to spawn," she explained. "Overfishing, concrete dams, polluted rivers, and hatchery fish contribute to the lowered numbers of North Pacific salmon. Unless we take drastic measures to preserve—and honor—the salmon, they may not exist for future generations."

Murphy holds a bachelor of arts degree from Santa Clara University and a master of fine arts degree in creative writing from the University of Alaska Fairbanks. She has taught writing on middle school through graduate levels and has published two books on Alaskan subjects for young people, *Friendship across Arctic Waters* and *To the Summit*. Murphy has lived in Alaska for 19 years with her husband and two children, Conor and Megan.

Duane Pasco was eager to contribute illustrations to this book because of "the importance of the Salmon People Legend and its connection to the art form and culture I so admire."

Born in Seattle, Pasco is self-taught and has been a professional artist in the contemporary Northwest Coast art form for 25 years. His traditional Indian carvings are held in private and museum collections throughout the world, including New York, Singapore, and Zaire. Neiman Marcus's famed Christmas catalog once featured his personalized totem poles as unique gift items.

Pasco is regarded as one of the most influential instructors in all aspects of the traditional art form. His vast knowledge shines through his illustrations for *Gyaehlingaay: Traditions, Tales, and Images of the Kaigani Haida* (1991), and in this, his first children's book. Pasco lives near Poulsbo, Washington, with his wife, Katie, and their three children.

To my brother Matt, with love. —CRM

To my wife Katie and our three children. Also to those master
native artists of the past who have been teachers by example.
—DP

This Tsimshian Indian version of the legend is adapted
from recordings made by anthropologists Franz Boas and
William Beynon in the early twentieth century.
Additional information was obtained through extensive
research about the Tsimshian people—their stories,
rituals, and traditional way of life—through personal
interviews with scholars and Tsimshian elders. Also, Cal
Skaugstad of the Alaska Department of Fish and
Game/Sport Fish provided information and clarification
on salmon migrations.

   The author wishes to gratefully thank traditional
Tsimshian artist Jack Hudson of Metlakatla for his
cultural and artistic assistance—he read the many drafts
of this manuscript. This book wouldn't have been
possible without him or the creative and cultural insights
of artist Duane Pasco and editor Kimberly Harbour, who
conceived the format of this book.

First published in the United States of America in 1993 by
RIZZOLI INTERNATIONAL PUBLICATIONS, INC.
300 Park Avenue South, New York NY 10010

Cataloging-in-Publication Data for this book
is available from the Library of Congress

ISBN: 0-8478-1662-1

Designed by José Conde
Edited by Kimberly Harbour

Cover illustration by Duane Pasco; back cover photo by Peter T. Furst,
Tlingit Salmon People, Lowie Museum of Anthropology, University of
California at Berkeley ; frontispiece photo by Maximilien Bruggmann,
Tsimshian shaman salmon charm, Canadian Museum of Civilization

Printed and bound in Hong Kong